Sorry To Hear About Your Kitty

By: Colleen Hollis

Illustrated and digitized by Colleen Hollis
Copyright © 2024 Colleen's Children Line Inc. Ltd.
Publisher: Colleen's Novels Inc. Ltd.
ISBN: 978-1-964768-01-4

I am so sorry to have heard about your beloved kitty cat_____,

You have come so far as a pet friend.

We are so proud of you, and appreciate all your efforts to care for your friend so well.

People may think it's all fun and play having a fur-friend.

It is actually consistent effort daily that makes someone a great caretaker.

Which is what you have been.

It is never easy to say goodbye to a fur-ever friend as loyal as yours.

We understand this time may be very difficult for you.

I can tell you, it will only feel
this way for now.

Please know it will get easier with support.

With time your tears will eventually turn into smiles as you think fondly back on your beloved kitty cat.

You will eventually look back and think of all the times your kitty made you laugh.

Or, recall how ornery your fur-friend was when going after your feet from around what seemed like every corner.

Remember all the crazy messes you've had to help clean up when your kitty was bored and would go bonkers.

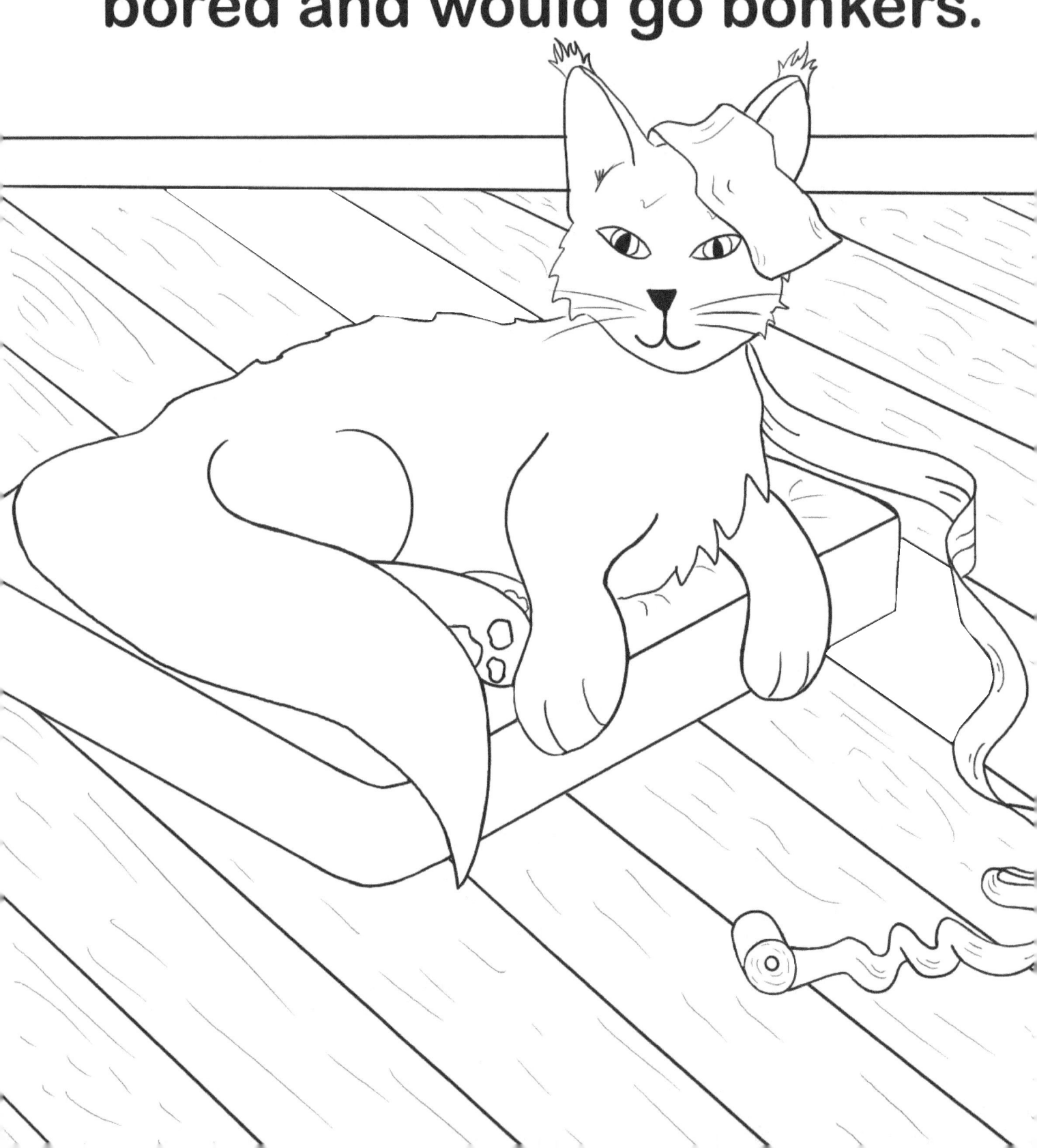

As independent as your kitty may have always been, it could most often be found by your side.

Or at other times, could be found looking over you from a distance.

Look within your heart and you'll see your friend is never far away.

Please know your kitty cat still loves you very much.

You are loved and supported forever and always.

Love, _____

Friend's Facts

Friend's Name:_____

Friend's Age:_____

Friend's Favorite Food/s:_____

_____

Friend's Favorite Activity:_____

_____

Friend's Favorite Toy/s: _____

_____

Friend's Favorite Person/s:_____

_____

Feel free to write a little note, or share a memory or two.

Sorry To Hear About Your Kitty, is one of the books in the children's line from Colleen's Bereavement Line For Children. Colleen's Bereavement Line for Children is aimed to assist in the healing process of children that find themselves navigating the loss of a loved one or pet. Sorry To Hear About Your Kitty focuses specifically on those with a kitty friend. A name can be added to the beginning of the book, while in the back of the book there is space to write memories about the fur-ever friend. Followed by a page for "Friend Facts" that can be filled in for a more personal feel.

All animal books in the series are interactive as well, they are in a coloring book format. Art has been shown as a useful tool that can aid in the healing process.